This Book Belongs To:

_____

Richard Scarry's
Busy Day Storybook Treasury

J-B Communications
Derrydale Books™
New York

This 2000 edition is published by J-B Communications, in conjunction with Derrydale Books™,
an imprint of Random House Value Publishing, Inc., 280 Park Avenue, New York, New York 10017.

Derrydale Books™ and design are trademarks of Random House Value Publishing, Inc.

Random House
New York • Toronto • London • Sydney • Auckland
http://www.randomhouse.com/

Printed and bound in China

Library of Congress Cataloging-in-Publicaton Data

Scarry, Richard.
   [Busy day storybook treasury]
   Richard Scarry's busy day storybook treasury.
      p. cm.
   Summary: Presents five stories about the busy and exciting activities of Humperdink
the pig, Mother Cat, Miss Honey, Sergeant Murphy, and the firefighters.
   ISBN 0-517-16226-1
   1. Children's stories, American. [1. Animals—Fiction. 2. Short stories.] I. Title: Busy
day storybook treasury. II. Title.

PZ7.S327 Rht 2000
[E]—dc21   00-029043

8 7 6 5 4 3 2 1

Contents

Humperdink's Busy Day

It is very early
in the morning.

All of Busytown
is still fast asleep.

8

"Drrinnng!" sounds the alarm clock next to Baker Humperdink's bed.

It is time for him to begin baking bread for hungry Busytowners!

Baker Humperdink rides off through the dark on his bicycle to the bakery.

Brushes drives by in his street sweeper.
"Good morning, Humperdink!" calls Brushes.
"Good morning, Brushes!" waves Humperdink.
Humperdink stops at Able Baker Charlie's house.

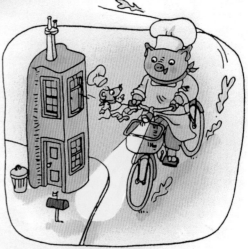

Able Baker Charlie hops onto Humperdink's bicycle.

On their way to the bakery, they pass
the TV bug reporters.
They are out to report the morning's
news.

11

At the bakery, Humperdink and Able Baker Charlie first warm up the oven.

While the oven gets hot, Humperdink kneads bread dough made from flour, water, salt and yeast.

Able Baker Charlie makes different-shaped loaves of bread out of the bread dough.

Good work, Charlie!

When the loaves are ready,
Humperdink and Able Baker
Charlie put them in the oven.

Now they must wait for the loaves
of bread to bake.

"What do you say
we have a donut
raffle today?"
Humperdink
asks Charlie.

Charlie agrees that it's a great idea.
He prepares the raffle tickets while
Humperdink makes the donuts.

Whoops! I think
the bread is
ready boys!

Humperdink and Able Baker
Charlie run to the oven.

They take out the baked bread just in time.
Ummm! Doesn't it smell delicious?

While the bread cools, they put the donuts into the oven.

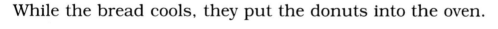

Once the loaves of bread have cooled, Humperdink places them in the bakery window.

Able Baker Charlie is going to make deliveries.
"Drive carefully, Charlie!" Humperdink says.

Charlie climbs onto his delivery bicycle and pedals away.

First he delivers long French baguettes to Louie's Restaurant.

"How are you today?"
Louie asks Charlie.
"Very well, thank you!"
replies Able Baker Charlie.

Charlie then brings bread to Hank's market.

"Have a nice day, Charlie!"
says Hank.
"Thanks, Hank!" says Charlie, pedaling away.

When Able Baker Charlie returns to the bakery, he sees the firefighters going inside.

"Have they come to buy some bread?" wonders Charlie.

NO! They have come to put out a burnt-donut fire! "Whooosh!" goes the firefighters' water hose.

When the fire is out, the firefighters leave the bakery.

"Don't forget to take a raffle ticket!" Humperdink says.

Humperdink starts to make a new batch of donuts.

Just then, Patience, the baby-sitter, arrives with little Sophie Humperdink.
"Could you please look after Sophie while I go to my dental appointment?" Patience asks Humperdink.
"No problem, Patience!" Humperdink says.

Both Humperdink and Able Baker Charlie are a little tired from getting up so early in the morning.

They decide to have a nap while the new donuts bake in the oven.

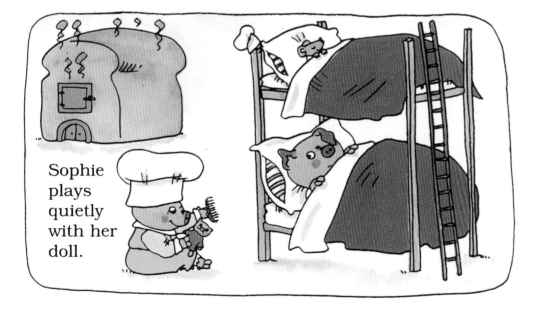

Sophie plays quietly with her doll.

21

Suddenly,
Humperdink is
awakened by
a strange noise.

Oh no! It's the firefighters again!

Humperdink and Able Baker
Charlie leap from their beds and take
the baked donuts out of the oven
just in time!

Good work, boys!

Now it is time for the raffle!
Humperdink reaches into his hat
to pull out the winning number.

He pulls out a ticket
and holds it up.

"The winning ticket..."
shouts Charlie,
"is number four!"

"That's OUR ticket!" says Smokey.
"We won the raffle!"

Baker Humperdink and Able Baker Charlie
bring out the big raffle prize.
The firefighters look very pleased.
They love to eat donuts.

The firefighters drive away with their prize.
"You know, Charlie," says Humperdink, "we haven't
eaten a *thing* all day!"
They decide to have a good meal at Louie's Restaurant.

... a big bowl of breadcrumb soup!

Their favorite!

Mother Cat's Busy Day

It is early in the morning, before the sun comes up. A light goes on in the Cat family house.

"Mommy, I'm hungry!" says Little Sally Cat.

For Mother Cat, it's the start of another busy day!

28

In the kitchen, Mother Cat
prepares breakfast for the Cat family.

While everyone eats,
she makes sandwiches
for Huckle's and
Lowly's lunchboxes.

29

It is time for the Cat Family to be on its way.
Mother Cat quickly loads the washing machine.

Father Cat goes out to the car through the back door. *BANG!*
Sally and Huckle follow him. *BANG! BANG!*
Then Lowly. *BANG!*

"Really," says Mother Cat, "I must
get that banging door repaired."

The Cat family drives away.

First, Mother Cat drops off
Huckle and Lowly at the
school bus stop.

"Goodbye, Mom!" waves Huckle.
"Goodbye, Mrs. Cat!" waves Lowly.
"Have fun at school today!" calls Mrs. Cat.

Then Mother Cat brings Sally
to the kindergarten.

Mrs. Murphy, the kindergarten teacher, awaits them.
"Welcome, Sally!" she says.
Mother Cat gives Sally a kiss, and then drives Father Cat
to the train station. He has an important business trip to
Workville today.

Now Mother Cat has some errands to run. By chance, she sees Mr. Fixit in his repair truck.

"Good morning, Mrs. Cat," says Mr. Fixit. "Can you please come over to our house and fix a banging back door?" Mother Cat asks Mr. Fixit. "Sure thing, Mrs. Cat!" Mr. Fixit replies. "There's nothing Mr. Fixit can't fix!"

While Mother Cat goes food shopping at the supermarket,
Mr. Fixit inspects the Cat's family back door.
"Hmmm," he says.

After shopping, Mother Cat takes a moment to rest at Mr. Raccoon's coffee shop.

"Good morning, Mrs. Cat," says Mr. Raccoon. "What can I bring you today?"
Mother Cat orders a cup of hot tea, and a bacon, lettuce, and tomato sandwich.

Meanwhile, Mr. Fixit starts to fix the Cat family back door. He removes the door with its hinges. **SPROING!**

He removes the doorframe from the wall.

He brings his biggest hammer from his repair truck.

Soon it is time for Mother Cat to pick up Sally from the kindergarten.

Sally has made a finger-painting for her mother. "Thank you, Sally," says Mother Cat, hugging her. "It's beautiful!"

Then she picks up Huckle and Lowly at the schoolbus stop. The boys have made Mother Cat a pencil-holder in class. "Thank you!" says Mother Cat. "This will be so useful by the telephone."

My!
Hasn't Mr. Fixit
been busy!
He pauses
to look at
his work.

Then he looks at the Cat family garage.
"Aha!" he says.

39

Mother Cat invites the children for sundaes at Bruno's ice-cream parlor. *Mmm!*

40

They have just enough time to finish
before fetching Father Cat at the train
station.

Father Cat has thoughtfully brought Mrs. Cat a bouquet of
flowers.
"I had such a successful day!" he says.
Mother Cat takes the flowers and gives him a kiss.

41

"After so much driving around today, I think the Cat family's car needs some gas!" says Mother Cat.

Mother Cat drives into Scottie's filling station.

Look! Mr. Fixit is filling up his truck, too! "Did you have any luck with that banging door?" Mrs. Cat asks Mr. Fixit.

42

"Did I ever!" replies Mr. Fixit. "I promise
you, that old door will never bang again."

43

My heavens, Mr. Fixit wasn't kidding! There surely is nothing that Mr. Fixit can't fix for good. Why, he has even built a new mailbox, swings for the children, and hung up Mrs. Cat's laundry to dry!

44

45

"Wow, this is great, Mom!" says Huckle. "We must be the only family in Busytown with a drive-in kitchen!"

46

The sun is up!
Miss Honey and Bruno wake from their sleep.

"Good morning, Bruno," says Miss Honey.
"Good morning, Miss Honey!" says Bruno, yawning.
"Did you sleep well?"

While Miss Honey
washes her face
and brushes her teeth
in the bathroom,
Bruno gets dressed.

Don't forget to wash,
too, Bruno!

Miss Honey and Bruno go to the kitchen.
Bruno sits down at the table.

"What would you like
for breakfast today, Bruno?"
Miss Honey asks.
"Chocolate ice cream, please!"
replies Bruno.

"But, Bruno," says Miss Honey, "you had chocolate ice cream for breakfast yesterday."

"Hmmm," thinks Bruno, "then today I'll have pistachio, OK?"

Bruno drives Miss Honey to school
in his ice cream truck.

At the school door,
she waves goodbye to him.
Soon schoolchildren arrive.

52

"Good morning, pupils!" Miss Honey says.
"Good morning, Miss Honey!" reply the children.

The children take their seats in the classroom,
and Miss Honey checks the attendance list.

"Hilda? Huckle? Lowly?... Vanderbuilt?" she asks.
"Where is Vanderbuilt?"

Aa Bb Cc Dd Ee Ff Gg Hh Ii Jj Kk Ll Mm Nn

Suddenly Vanderbuilt appears in the door.
"Excuse me for being late, Miss Honey," Vanderbuilt says,
"Uncle Gronkle's car wouldn't start this morning!"

54

First, the class practices spelling.
"Who knows how to spell APPLE?"
asks Miss Honey.

Pp Qq Rr Ss Tt Uu Vv Ww Xx Yy Zz

Lowly spells, "A-P-P-L-E, apple!"
Good for you, Lowly!

Next, the class works with numbers.
Miss Honey asks Vanderbuilt to do
an addition.
Miss Honey is patient and helps
Vanderbuilt find the answer.

The class bell rings.
It's time for gym!

The pupils leave the classroom
to change into their sports uniforms
in the locker room.

The class plays a game of basketball with Mr. Tough. It's lots of fun!

Flossy Bunny shoots the ball into the net.

Good shot, Flossy!

After gym, it's time for lunch. The children join Miss Honey in the school cafeteria. There are many different things to choose from.

"Try to choose items from more than one food group," Miss Honey says. "That's the way to keep healthy!"

59

Then it's time for recess.
While everyone plays outside
in the school playground,
Miss Honey gives Bruno
a telephone call.

"What did you have
for lunch today, Bruno?"
Miss Honey asks.
"Ice cream!" replies Bruno.

"Bruno, you have to eat
something other than
just ice cream!" says
Miss Honey.
"Okay, Miss Honey, I
promise. Tomorrow I will
eat something different."

61

This afternoon, Miss Honey has a special treat for her class: a field trip to the Busytown Fire Station!

The class rides to the firehouse in the school bus.

Smokey greets
them at the door.

"Wow!" says Huckle. "This is neat!"

The children learn all about the fire truck
and the firefighters' duties, and Snozzle
brings everyone refreshments.

As a surprise, the firefighters drive the class back to school in the fire engine.

Aren't they lucky! I think Miss Honey enjoys the return ride, too.

Back in the classroom, Miss Honey asks the pupils to make a drawing of the fire station to bring in to school tomorrow.

The school bell rings, and Miss Honey's class heads home.
What a busy day it has been! Look! Here comes Bruno!
He has brought Miss Honey a rose.

"May I invite you out to dinner tonight, Miss Honey?" he asks. "Why, I'd be delighted. Thank you!" says Miss Honey. "Where shall we go?"

65

Why, of course, to Bruno's favorite:
the ice cream parlor!

Sergeant Murphy's Busy Day

Well before the sun is up, Sergeant Murphy's telephone
rings. "DRRINNNG!!!" Sergeant Murphy wakes up.
"Hello?" he answers the telephone, "Sergeant Murphy here."
It is Deputy Flo calling from the police station.

"I have looked everywhere,
Sergeant Murphy," she says,
"but I can't find your
whistle! You can't work
today without it!"

"Don't worry, Flo," answers
Sergeant Murphy.
"My whistle is right here
beside me. Thanks
for calling!"

The Murphy family gets up for another busy day.

While Mrs. Patsy Murphy dresses little Bridget, Sergeant Murphy prepares breakfast.

Umm! Don't those eggs and bacon smell good?

Soon it is time for Sergeant Murphy and Bridget to go.

"Goodbye!"

Sergeant Murphy drives Bridget to the
kindergarten in his motorcycle's sidecar.

On the way, his motorcycle telephone begins to ring.
"DRRINNNG! DRRINNNG!"

It's Mrs. Murphy on
the line.

"Sarge, you left your
whistle behind this
morning, but don't
worry, I will leave it
at the police station."

Sergeant Murphy
drops Bridget off at
kindergarten.
"Bye, Daddy!" calls
Bridget, as she enters.
"Goodbye, Bridget!
Have fun!" calls
Sergeant Murphy.

"DRRINNNG!" goes Sergeant
Murphy's telephone.
It's Mayor Fox calling.
"Sergeant Murphy, there is a
giant traffic jam outside.
Busytown needs your help to
clear it up!"

"Yes sir, Mayor Fox!"
replies Sergeant
Murphy. "I'm on my
way!"

But Sergeant Murphy wonders how he will direct traffic without his whistle.

Just then, he sees a band playing in the park. He stops and asks if he may borrow the cymbals.

With the cymbals tucked neatly in his sidecar, he speeds away.

My, what a traffic jam!
"Just stay calm, everybody!" Sergeant Murphy says.

"Clang!" Sergeant Murphy directs cars to the left.
"Clang!" he directs cars to the right.
The traffic jam is sorted out.

Good work!

Directing traffic makes Sergeant Murphy hungry.
He stops for a donut and hot chocolate at Humperdink's
bakery.

His telephone rings.

"DRRINNNG! DRRINNNG!" It's Deputy Flo, calling from
the police station.

"Mrs. Murphy has brought your whistle!" says Flo.

"Thank you, Flo!" answers Sergeant Murphy. "I'll be over soon to fetch it."

But before he can finish his donut, his telephone rings again!

Why, it's little Sophie Pig. She is crying! While she was shopping with her mother at the supermarket, she got lost.

"Don't worry, Sophie!" says Sergeant Murphy.
"I'm on my way!"
Before you can say "hot chocolate," he's off!

VRROOOM!

On the way, Sergeant Murphy's telephone rings again! It's Sophie's mother on the line. She, too, is crying! She can't find her daughter anywhere in the supermarket!

"Just stay calm!" Sergeant Murphy says. "I will find her for you."

At the supermarket, Sergeant Murphy finds Sophie and brings her to her mother. Thank goodness for Sergeant Murphy!

Sergeant
Murphy
looks at
his watch.
It's time
to give a
traffic-safety
lesson at
school!

"DRRINNNG!" sounds Sergeant Murphy's telephone.
It's Deputy Flo again.
"Sergeant Murphy, since you didn't come for your whistle,
I'm leaving it at Humperdink's bakery."
"Thank you, Flo," says Sergeant Murphy.

On his way to school, Sergeant Murphy wonders how
he will instruct the children without his whistle.
But he gets an idea and borrows Huckle's bicycle bell.

"Ring! Ring!
Stop!" directs
Sergeant Murphy.
"Ring! Ring! GO!"

That's a pretty funny police whistle, Sergeant Murphy!

It is time for Sergeant Murphy
to coach the school's soccer
team.

Without his whistle to coach the
team, Sergeant Murphy borrows a
school band tuba.
Huckle kicks the soccer ball high in
the sky, but no one sees it come
down again.

"That ball went out of
bounds!" says Sergeant
Murphy.
He tries to blow the tuba,
but no sound comes out.
He blows harder...

"TOOOOT!" sounds the tuba, as the soccer ball flies out.

"That sure is the funniest coaching whistle I've ever seen!" laughs Huckle.

"But it works!" answers Sergeant Murphy, "TOOOOT!!!"

After soccer practice, Sergeant Murphy drives to pick up Bridget at the kindergarten.

"Hi, Daddy!" she waves. "Have you had a busy day?"

"Oh, yes," replies Sergeant Murphy, "and my busy day is not yet finished!"
Sergeant Murphy drives with Bridget to Humperdink's bakery to pick up his whistle.

Able Baker Charlie
is there to greet them.

"I'm sorry, Sergeant
Murphy," Charlie says,
"Baker Humperdink just
left, and he took your
whistle with him!"
Poor Sergeant Murphy.

Just then, the telephone rings.

84

"It's for you!" says Charlie,
handing Sergeant Murphy the telephone.

It's Mrs. Murphy.

"Could you come
home soon, please,
Sarge? It's important!"
"Okay, Patsy!" he
replies. "We're on
our way home!"

What a surprise! Baker Humperdink, Sophie, Sophie's mother, Flo, and even Able Baker Charlie are there. Baker Humperdink hands Sergeant Murphy his whistle. "Thank you for having found our little Sophie today! I've baked you this whistle cake!" he says.

"My, that's the funniest cake I've ever seen," says Sergeant Murphy, "but won't it taste good!"

The Firefighters' Busy Day

All is quiet inside
the Busytown Firehouse
early in the morning.
Snozzle, Smokey,
Sparky and Squirty sleep
soundly in their beds.

"Drrinnng!!!"
sounds the fire alarm.

The four firefighters jump from
their beds, put on their helmets,
and slide down the pole.
The fire engine waits downstairs.

Hurry,
firefighters!

The fire engine races through the streets.
"Clang! Clang!" goes the bell.
"Toot! Toot!" sounds Sparky's horn.

Make way, everybody!

90

They arrive at
Mr. Frumble's
house.
My! Look at all
that smoke!

Smokey, Sparky, Squirty and Snozzle burst through the door, fire hose in hand.

Mr. Frumble is preparing burnt toast for breakfast. Yum. Yum.

The firefighters drive back to the firehouse and sit down for breakfast.

Smokey prepares pancakes.

"Drrinnng!!!" sounds the alarm again.

Sorry, firefighters! Breakfast will have to wait!

Off drive
the firefighters
to the rescue.

It's Mr. Frumble again.
His pickle car key
has fallen into
the gutter.
Smokey pulls it out
with a magnet.

The firefighters return
to the firehouse
to eat cold pancakes.

"Drrinnng!!!" sounds the alarm
once again.

The firetruck speeds once again to the rescue.

Guess who needs help? Mr. Frumble should learn to drive more carefully, don't you think?

Smokey turns off the fire
hydrant, and Mr. Frumble
and his pickle car
land softly
on the street.

The firefighters
return to the
firehouse.

They
decide
to grill
hot dogs.

"Drrinnng!!!"
goes
the alarm.

96

The firefighters race
to the rescue again.

Uh-oh. Now
Mr. Frumble
has lost his
hat in a tree.

Using a ladder, the firefighters fetch Mr. Frumble's hat and give it back to him.

"Drrinnng! Drrinnng!" goes the telephone on the firetruck. Smokey answers the phone. It's another alarm.

It's a FIRE!

The firefighters
hurry through the streets.

"Clang! Clang!"
"Toot! Toot!"
Watch out,
everybody!

Smoke billows out of a garage door. Squirty shoots
the water cannon. Sparky runs forward with the hose.
Hurry, firefighters!

"Whooosh!!!" With a spray of water,
the fire is out in an instant.

101

"Drrinnng!!!"
sounds
the alarm.

Without wasting a minute,
the firefighters are off
to the next emergency.
Poor, hungry firefighters!

They arrive at Mr. Frumble's house again.
Mr. Frumble is having a bath.

I think your bathtub is full now, Mr. Frumble.

So that they can finally have a quiet moment
to eat, the firefighters invite Mr. Frumble to
have dinner with them at the firehouse.

Squirty stirs
a big pot of
firefighter
stew.

Sparky
brings out the bowls.

Everyone sits down at the table.
Doesn't the stew smell good!

The firefighters are off to the next rescue.
My, don't firefighters have a busy day!

Oh, bon appétit, Mr. Frumble!

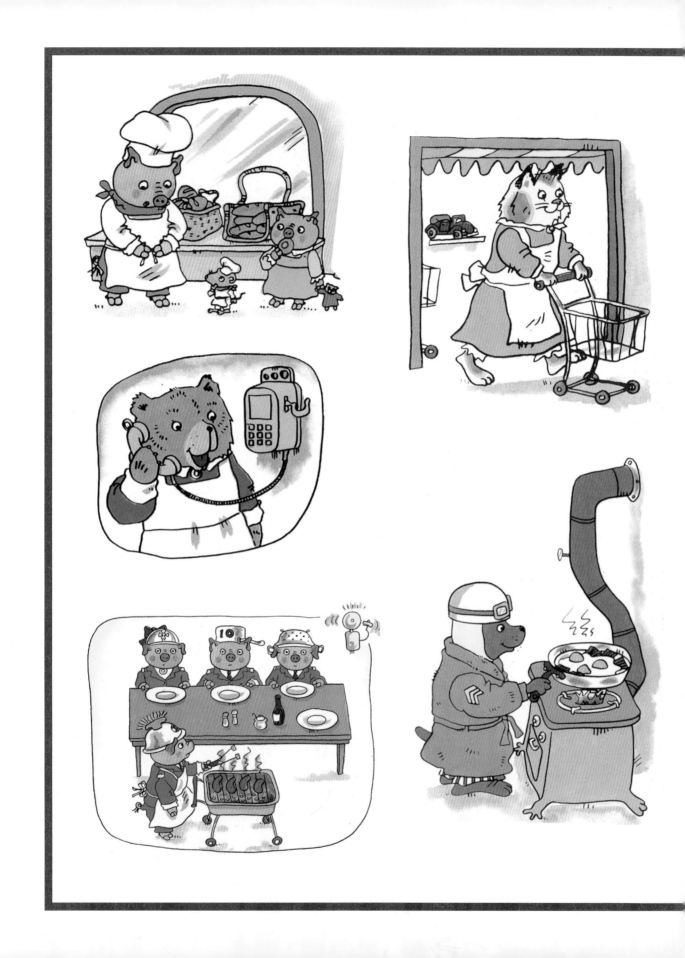